CHESS

Claire Summerscale

DK

LONDON, NEW YORK, MUNICH,
MELBOURNE, AND DELHI

Senior editor Claire Nottage
Senior art editor Stefan Podhorodecki
Designer Spencer Holbrook
Illustrator Nikid Design Ltd
Managing editor Linda Esposito
Managing art editor Diane Thistlethwaite
Publishing managers Caroline Buckingham
and Andrew Macintyre
Category publisher Laura Buller
Production controller Katherine Thornton
DTP designer Siu Chan
Jacket editor Mariza O'Keeffe
Jacket designer Stefan Podhorodecki
Consultant Aaron Summerscale

First published in Great Britain in 2006 by
Dorling Kindersley Limited,
80 Strand,
London WC2R 0RL

2 4 6 8 10 9 7 5 3 1

Copyright © 2006 Dorling Kindersley Limited, London
A Penguin Company

ISBN-13: 978-1-4053-1326-1
ISBN-10: 1-4053-1326-9

Colour reproduction by Icon Reproduction, London
Printed in China by Hung Hing Offset Printing Co. Ltd

Discover more at
www.dk.com

CONTENTS

The game of chess

Many countries, including China, India, and Persia, claim to have invented chess, but noone knows for certain where the game originated. Over the centuries its popularity grew, and the game spread around the globe. In 1866, Wilhelm Steinitz won the first official world championships held in London. Since then, there have been many world champions, and today chess is still the oldest and most popular game of skill in the world.

Persian painting depicting a chess game

◄ The origin of the pieces

Originally, the chess set contained an elephant instead of a bishop and a prime minister instead of a a queen. Later, the Europeans changed the names and designs of the pieces to reflect their own lives. Similarly, in some places in the world today, the rook is referred to as "the elephant" and the bishop as "the camel".

◄ The Lewis chess set

In 1831, on the coast of the Isle of Lewis, in the Outer Hebrides, a very old chess set was discovered. The pieces are considered to be the earliest examples of a European set and are thought to have been made in Norway in about AD 1200. They are now on display in the British Museum in London.

The king from the Lewis chess set

► The Staunton set

Differences in language, culture, and wealth meant that chess sets became very varied, so much so that when players from different countries competed against each other, they were confused by the pieces. Then, in the 1840s, John Jaques of London became the first company to produce a universally recognizable chess set. It became known as the Staunton set, named after Howard Staunton, an English chess master.

▶ Computer chess

Computers have changed the way chess is played dramatically. The earliest chess computer programs developed in the 1950s were very basic. By 1996, a powerful supercomputer named Deep Blue defeated the then world chess champion Garry Kasparov. Today, computers can help players analyse any chess position or game. They also enable chess enthusiasts in different countries to play each other online.

Garry Kasparov plays Deep Junior, the successor of Deep Blue

▶ DK chess set

This book features specially commissioned, computer-generated pieces, based on the traditional Staunton set. The pieces are animated throughout the book to reflect their situations.

Silver king from the DK set

Chess is a game for all ages

▶ A game for everyone

Chess is a game of infinite possibilities, and has captured the imagination and attention of millions of players since its invention. This book will teach you all you need to know about learning to play chess, and you will quickly discover how to outwit your opponent every time!

The traditional Staunton chess set

CHAPTER ONE:

Introduction

CONTENTS

The object of the game

You can think of chess as a battle between two armies. One player controls the white army and the other player controls the black army. Each army has 16 soldiers, which vary in strength and importance. The ultimate aim is to trap and checkmate the king, since checkmate, or the death of the king, ends the game.

King
The king is the commander of the army.

Queen
The queen is an extremely powerful attacking and defensive piece.

Bishop
The bishops stand on either side of the king and queen and move diagonally around the board.

Rook
The rooks protect the king on the back rank and can move speedily around the board.

Knight
The two knights stand beside the bishops and move in a unique way.

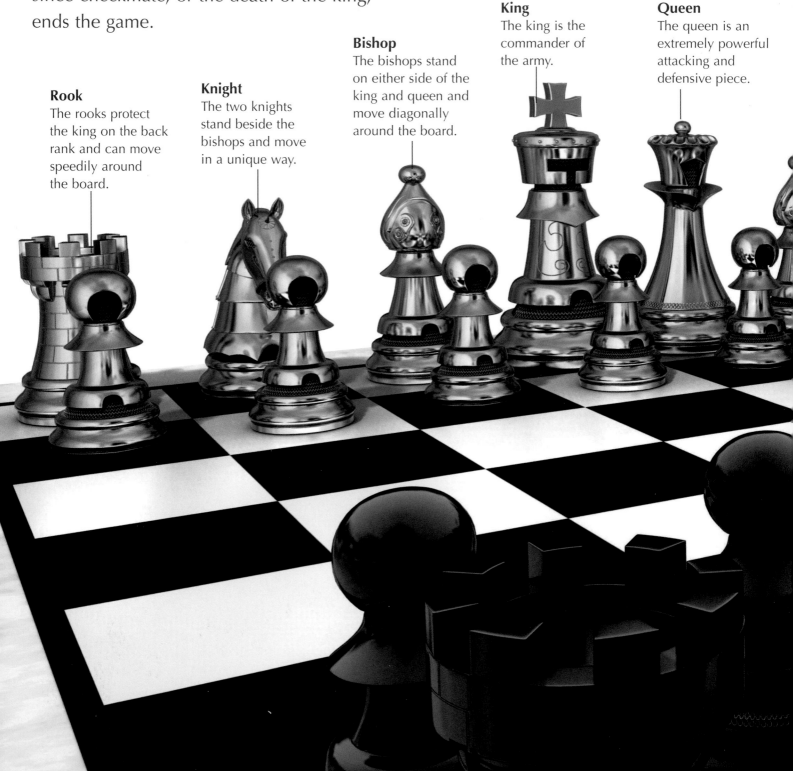

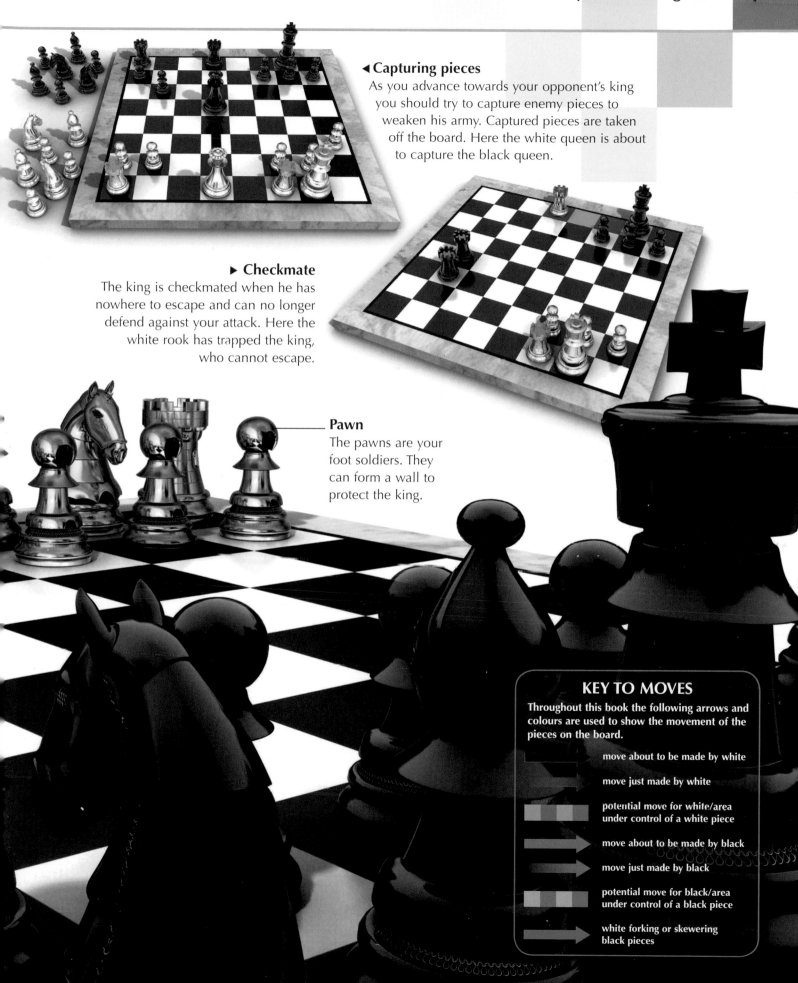

◄ Capturing pieces
As you advance towards your opponent's king you should try to capture enemy pieces to weaken his army. Captured pieces are taken off the board. Here the white queen is about to capture the black queen.

► Checkmate
The king is checkmated when he has nowhere to escape and can no longer defend against your attack. Here the white rook has trapped the king, who cannot escape.

Pawn
The pawns are your foot soldiers. They can form a wall to protect the king.

KEY TO MOVES
Throughout this book the following arrows and colours are used to show the movement of the pieces on the board.

move about to be made by white

move just made by white

potential move for white/area under control of a white piece

move about to be made by black

move just made by black

potential move for black/area under control of a black piece

white forking or skewering black pieces

Starting positions

Chess is played on a board with eight columns called files, each containing eight squares, and eight rows, or ranks, also containing eight squares. So in total, there are 64 squares on every chess board. You need to set up the pieces in their correct positions before you start.

▲ SETTING UP YOUR PIECES

The back row is always set up like this, with the king and queen in the middle, a bishop on either side of them, then the knights, then the rooks.

◄ READY TO PLAY

This is how your board will look when you are ready to start. The board must always have the white square in the bottom right-hand corner. Remember, white must be on the right! Also remember that the queen always starts on her own colour – the white queen on a white square, the black queen on a black square.

QUEENSIDE   KINGSIDE

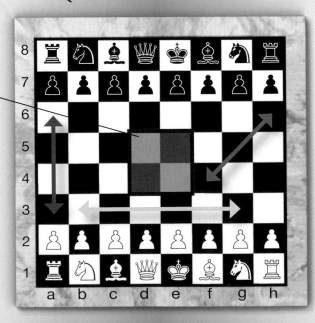

The centre squares are important since, if occupied, they enable a piece to have control over the whole board

squares running from top to bottom are called files

squares running diagonally are called diagonals

squares running from left to right are called ranks

◄ HOW THE BOARD WORKS

This is how the board looks when it is presented in notation form (see opposite). The board is divided into two sides – queenside and kingside. You will come across these terms later in the book.

Chess notation

Every square on a chess board has its identity. Each piece has its own outline shape which you will see used in chess quizzes on computers and in newspapers. Each piece is also represented by a letter, which is used when the moves are written down.

A chess board has a grid system for writing down moves

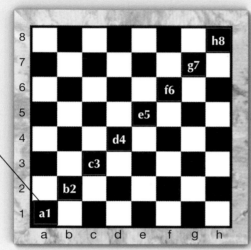

▲ Grid system
Every square is named according to its position on the board. The ranks are named a-h and the files 1-8.

Writing down moves
When you start to play proper chess games, you will need to write your moves down on a score sheet. When you do this, you have to indicate which piece has moved to which square and also show extra information such as check and castling. You will learn about these moves later on in this book. White always moves first.

White	Black
1 e4	e5
2 Qh5	Nc6
3 Bc4	g6
4 Qf3	Qh4
5 Qxf7+	

SCORE SHEET

K

King

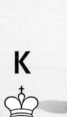 **Q**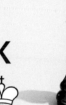

Queen

B

Bishop

 R

Rook

 **N**

Knight

Pawn

▲ Identifying pieces
Each piece is usually represented in outline on a chess board. When moves are written down, each piece is identified by a letter, apart from the pawn which has no letter. For example, a rook moving to d3 is written as Rd3, whereas a pawn moving to d3 would just be written as d3.

Advanced notation

Different types of moves are written down in a specific form. Kingside castling is written as 0-0 and queenside castling is written as 0-0-0. Capturing is indicated by an "x" and if the move puts the king in check, a "+" is added. Look at this example below.

If the white bishop took the black pawn on f7 it would be written as Bxf7+. This shows that the bishop captured (x) a piece on f7 and that he has put the black king in check (+).

CHAPTER TWO:

The pieces

CONTENTS

The rook

When you first start playing chess you will sometimes hear other people say that the rooks are also called castles. Although they look like castles, more experienced players will always call them rooks. Rooks are very valuable in a game of chess, so they are referred to as major pieces.

◄ **How does the rook move?**
Rooks move in straight lines, up and down the files or side to side across the ranks. They can move as many squares as they want to in a straight line.

▶ **Capturing**
Rooks can never jump over any other pieces, so if an enemy soldier is in their way, they must either stop, or capture it. This white rook can move straight up the board and capture the black rook on d8.

MASTER TIPS

Using open lines

A line can be described as open when it is not blocked by either friendly or enemy pawns. Rooks are in their element in these situations – they love open lines. On this board, the power of the rook on b1 is severely reduced by the b2 pawn, but the g1 rook is not blocked and is free to roam up and down the board to his heart's content!

The g1 rook is far superior to the rook on b1 due to the open g-file.

 Do
capture as many of your opponent's pieces as you can during the course of a game.

 Don't
take your own pieces, because this would be an illegal move.

DID YOU KNOW?
Italians call the rook *rocco* ("small fortress"), a version of the Persian name for the piece, *rukh*.

Capturing practice

It is essential that you get used to the way each of the pieces moves and captures. The best way to do this and become a chess expert is to practise on your own board. Have a look at these two diagrams. Can you set up these positions on your board and work out the answers to these tricky questions? Remember that your rooks move up and down and side to side.

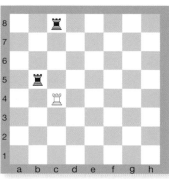

1. Which black piece can the white rook capture? Is it the black rook on b5 or c8?

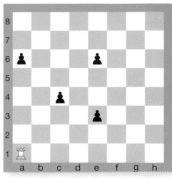

2. Your rook can capture these pawns in five moves. Don't worry if it takes more moves at first. Keep practising!

Rooks resemble castle turrets which is why they are sometimes called castles

Double trouble ▶

Your rooks can move around the board quickly and can be particularly useful if you use them in pairs.

The bishop

The piece we now know as the bishop originated in India and would have appeared as an elephant in an Indian chess set. When chess arrived in the west, European players remodelled the piece to represent a member of the church clergy, who used to hold positions of great power in royal courts.

The bishop is clearly identified by his mitre – the hat worn by church bishops

▲ How does the bishop move?
Bishops move diagonally, as many squares as they want to at a time, both forwards and backwards. They always stay on their starting colour.

▲ Capturing
Bishops can't jump over any other pieces. If another piece is in his way, the bishop must either stop before he reaches that piece, or capture it. Here, the white bishop can capture the black rook.

Stay on your squares

At the start of the game, you have two bishops. One moves on the light squares, the other on the dark squares. Bishops always stay on the colour that they started on. If you end up with both of your bishops on the same coloured square, you know that something has gone wrong and that you have moved one of your bishops like a banana!

Your bishops must always stay on the same coloured squares that they start the game on.

 Do
concentrate on sticking to your diagonals.

 Don't
block your bishops in with your pawns.

▲ **Good bishop, bad bishop**
If a bishop is blocked in by his own pawns, he is described as a bad bishop. Here the white bishop is limited by the white pawns, but the black bishop can move easily all around the board.

 DID YOU KNOW?
The bishop was originally known as *Pil*, which means "elephant" in Arabic.

◄ **Strong teamwork**
Your light- and dark-squared bishops are a great double act – together they can control large areas of the board.

Diagonal dilemma

Remember that the bishops have to stay on the same diagonal and have a look at these boards.

1. Which black rook can the white bishop capture?

2. How many squares can the white bishop move to? Which piece can the white bishop capture?

The queen

The queen is extremely powerful and the only chess piece that represents a woman. At the start of the battle she stands next to her king and although it may be tempting to leave her to protect the king, it is better to use her strength to attack the enemy forces.

◀ **How does the queen move?**
The queen moves like the rook and bishop combined. She can move in straight lines like the rook and diagonally like the bishop.

▶ **Capturing**
The queen can move forwards and backwards, but she can never jump over any other pieces, so if an enemy soldier is in her way, she must either stop before she reaches that piece, or capture it.

MASTER TIPS

Look after your queen

At the start of the game, the queen usually controls her army from the back of the board – it's important to develop your other pieces before launching an attack with your queen. She is a very strong piece but she needs to be supported by the other troops. Remember that she always has the advantage over other pieces because she can move both in straight lines and on diagonals.

1. It is sensible to leave the queen on her starting square until most of your pieces have been developed.

2. If the queen captures the rook, the bishop will take her, so she should capture the bishop instead.

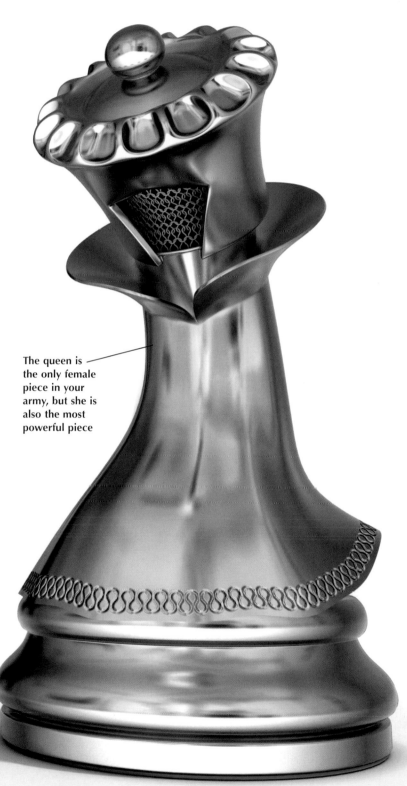

The queen is the only female piece in your army, but she is also the most powerful piece

Beware the lady ▲

The queen moves quickly and ruthlessly around the board and can obliterate any pieces in her path, so always be aware of her position.

 Do

remember that your queen is the most powerful piece on the board.

 Don't

develop your queen too early on in the game.

DID YOU KNOW?
The queen was introduced to the game in 1475. Elsewhere in the world she is called "The Lady".

MASTER CHALLENGE

Queen of carnage

Remember to pay special attention whenever you move this very important lady, as without the strength of his queen, the king can often end up in serious trouble!

1. Which black piece can the queen safely take here?

2. The queen needs to be careful. Which black piece can she capture safely this time?

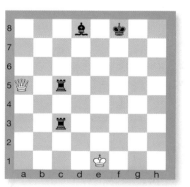

The knight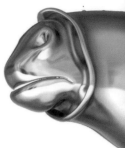

On a chess board, the knight is often depicted as a horse's head. The knight represents the medieval professional soldier, who protected people of higher rank, like the king and the queen. Just as knights held a special place in the court of King Arthur, knights are also special in the game of chess.

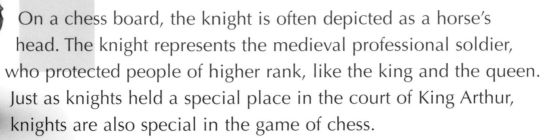

◄ How does the knight move?

The knight is the only piece that is allowed to jump over other pieces. He moves in an L-shape. Two squares in one direction and then one square to the side.

Knights in action ►

At the start of the game, your two knights are brilliant enough to be able to control all four central squares.

► Capturing

Hippedy-hippedy-hop is another way to describe how the knight moves, as he can hop or jump over other pieces, just as a horse would. He can only capture a piece on the hop, when he finally lands.

DID YOU KNOW?
The horses ridden by medieval knights wore armour on their bodies to protect them in battle.

◄ Getting stuck

Although the knight has the magic power to jump over other chess men, sometimes he can still get stuck. Here, the white knight has been blocked in by other white pieces. As you can never land on or capture one of your own pieces, the knight will have to wait patiently until they move out of his way.

Knights can leap over other pieces and make captures when you might not be expecting it!

Dim knights

We know that a knight can move to eight different squares from the centre of the board, but if he sits on the edge, he loses half of his power.

Here, the knight on a5 can only make four possible moves rather than his usual eight so he is half as powerful. This is why we say, knights on the rim are dim!

✓ Do

remember your knights have the useful skill of jumping over other pieces.

✗ Don't

put your knights in the corners or on the side of the board.

Get to know your knights

Your knights can be very useful but it can be tricky getting used to the way they move because they are very different from the other pieces. Once you have mastered their moves, you will begin to see quite how useful they can be and start to outwit your opponent with some crafty moves and captures. Have a look at these two boards.

1. On which square is the piece the knight can capture? Remember you cannot capture your own pieces.

2. See if you can capture both black pawns with your knight in six moves. It might take you longer at first.

The pawn

Your pawns are your infantry, or foot soldiers. Because they are on foot, they move slowly and can't escape easily from more powerful pieces. There are more pawns on the board than any other piece and they can be sacrificed to open up lines of attack.

◄ How does the pawn move?
In general, pawns can only move one square straight forwards, except on their first move, when, if they wish, they can move two squares straight forwards.

▶ Capturing
Unlike the other pieces, the pawn does not capture in the same way as it moves. Pawns can only capture other pieces by moving one square diagonally forwards, to the right or the left. The white pawn is moving up the board and the black pawn is moving down the board.

This pawn can capture the black knight or the black pawn. Equally, if it was black's move, the black pawn could capture the white pawn

MASTER TIPS

Pawn practice

It is always a good idea to play the pawn game with a friend so you can practise moving and capturing with the pawn. Start with the pawns in this position. The winner is the player who captures all of their opponent's pieces or gets a pawn to the end of the board. White always moves first – you can toss a coin to decide who plays white.

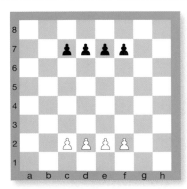

Remember the white corner square must be on your right!

 Do
remember that pawns can never move or capture backwards.

 Don't
move more than two or three pawns in the opening stages of the game.

 DID YOU KNOW?
The name of the pawn comes from *padati*, the Indian word used for a foot soldier in the game.

Queening a pawn

If a pawn reaches the other side of the board, something magical happens. Your foot soldier is rewarded by being promoted. He can transform himself into another piece: knight, bishop, rook, or queen. We know how valuable the queen is and therefore most players choose to change their pawn into another queen.

White can queen this d7 pawn by moving it to d8

White could also queen this pawn on f7 by capturing the black bishop on g8

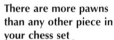

There are more pawns than any other piece in your chess set

Army of pawns ▶
Your army of pawns may move slowly but if they perform their duties well, they can be promoted to a higher rank.

MASTER CHALLENGE

Working your soldiers

Work those foot soldiers! What do you think is white's best move in these positions?

1. What would be white's best capture here?

2. What should white's next move be in this situation?

The king

The king is the most important piece on the board, as the object of the game is to trap your opponent's king. This means that you must protect your king at all times. The downfall of the king, as in days of old, means your opponent has won the battle.

▶ **How does the king move?**
Although the king is the most important piece on the board, he moves very slowly. He can only move one square in any direction: forwards, backwards, left, right, or diagonally.

▲ **Capturing**
The king captures pieces in the same way that he moves – he can take any enemy piece that is standing next to him.

▼ **Check**
When the king is attacked by an enemy piece we say that he is in check. The king can never stay on or move to a square where he could be captured by an enemy piece.

Here the black rook is attacking the white king

MASTER TIPS

The three rules of check

There are just three ways that you can escape from check – make sure you remember them!

1. Capture the checking piece.

2. Block the check. Put one of your pieces between the checking piece and your king.

3. Move your king out of the way and out of check.

1. The white king cannot move to a safe square but the e4 bishop can capture the checking rook.

2. The white rook can block the check by moving to d1.

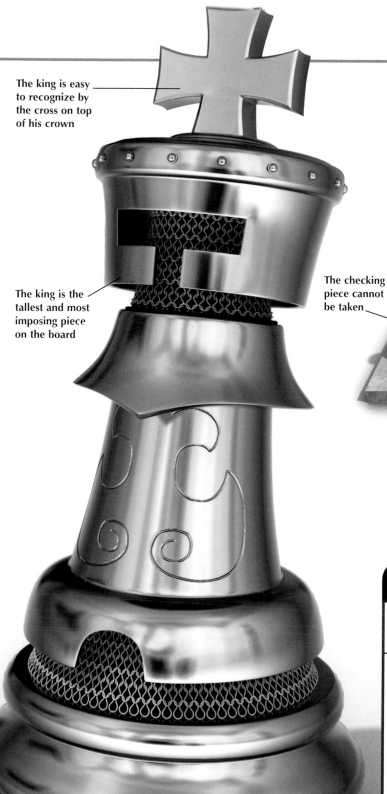

The king is easy to recognize by the cross on top of his crown

The king is the tallest and most imposing piece on the board

King and commander ▲

Because he moves so slowly the king is not very powerful. He cannot escape the enemy quickly and relies on his loyal army to protect him against attack.

▼ Checkmate

If you cannot escape from check using any of the three rules of check (*see* below, left), then you are in checkmate and the game is over. The word checkmate comes from the Persian words *shah mata* which mean "the king is dead". Here the white king cannot escape from the black queen and so the game is over.

The checking piece cannot be taken

The check cannot be blocked

None of the squares the white king could move to are safe

DID YOU KNOW?
Until the 13th century, all the squares on the chess board were the same colour.

MASTER CHALLENGE

Lead white to victory

Can you find the checkmating move for white in this game? White needs to find an immediate checkmate, as black has the deadly threat of queen to g2, checkmate.

The white knight plays a vital part in this checkmate

White can deliver checkmate by moving the queen on c7, but where should she move to?

Special moves

There are two special moves in chess which you must master. Castling can only be done once in a game and involves moving the rook and the king for the king's protection. En passant is an alternative method of capturing with a pawn. Both are very useful moves.

Your king is castled in order to protect him behind a wall of pawns

Castling your king

1 When you castle, your king first has to move two squares towards the rook. Here the white king is going to castle kingside (on the king's side of the board).

2 Once the king has moved, the rook flies over him and lands next to him. The white king has castled kingside, whereas the black king has castled queenside (on the queen's side of the board).

When can you not castle?

Always bear these five rules in mind. You cannot castle if you:
1. Have already moved your king or the involved rook.
2. Are in check.
3. Have to move your king into check when you castle.
4. Have to move through check when you castle.
5. Have any pieces in between the king and involved rook.

1. Here, the white king cannot castle because he is in check and the white rook has already moved.

2. Here, the white king can't castle as he would be moving through check from the black f5 rook.

The black pawn is waiting to capture the white pawn

Capturing en passant

1 *En passant* is French for "in passing" since although your opponent's pawn has passed the square where you would usually make a capture, you are still able to take it. Here, white has just moved his pawn two squares forward and has landed next to the black pawn.

2 Black has now taken this pawn on d4 but actually lands one square forward on d3. The white pawn has been captured en passant. Remember, an en passant move has to be made as soon as your opponent's pawn has moved two squares forward.

Black captures the white pawn next to it but lands one square forward

One pawn can capture another using the en passant move

 Do

castle your king as soon as possible. He is much safer on the side of the board.

 Don't

leave your king in the centre of the board – he must always be protected.

 Don't

forget that although you will not capture en passant very often, it is still an important move to master.

CHAPTER THREE:

Winning your first games

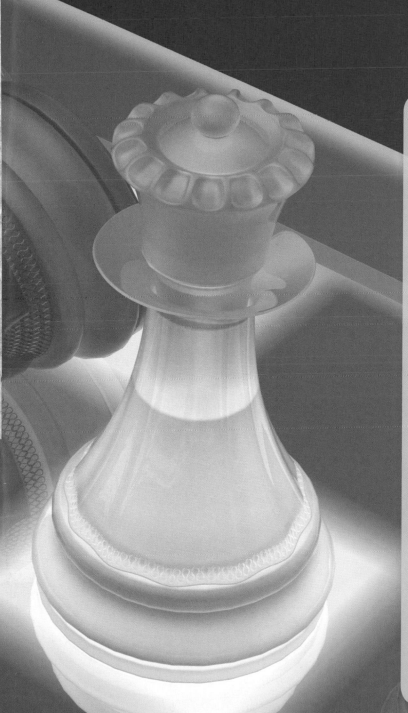

CONTENTS

Piece value and exchanging

As your game progresses, you will find opportunities to capture your opponent's pieces. However, your opponent may well recapture your men – this is known as exchanging. Therefore it is vital that you know the value of each piece, so you can ensure that you exchange wisely.

◄ The King
The king cannot be exchanged, but if he is checkmated, the game is lost, so we could say that the king is worth an infinite number of points.

◄ The Queen (9 points)
The queen is your most valuable piece. You should always guard her carefully and ensure she stays out of danger.

◄ Rooks (5 points each)
Because they can cover so many squares, rooks are more valuable than knights and bishops.

◄ Bishops (3 points each)
Bishops can move quickly across the whole board, but they are only worth three points each.

◄ Knights (3 points each)
Knights have the special talent of being able to jump over other pieces, but they are only worth three points.

◄ Pawns (1 point each)
If you have to make a sacrifice, you would lose the least by sacrificing a pawn.

A good exchange ▶
Here, white will gain five points if he captures the rook on a8 and will only lose three points if his bishop is recaptured by the other rook on f8. This is a good exchange for white.

Because rooks are worth more than bishops, white is happy to capture the black rook

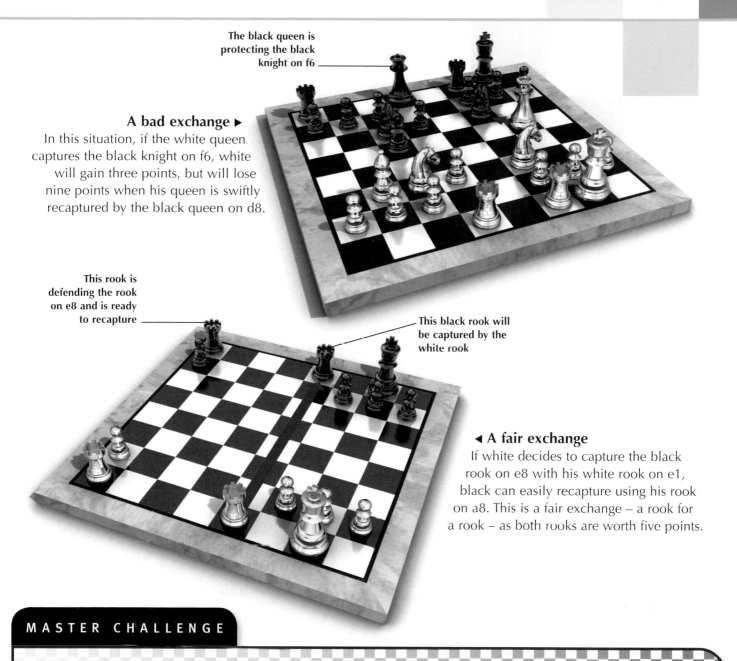

The black queen is
protecting the black
knight on f6

A bad exchange ▶
In this situation, if the white queen
captures the black knight on f6, white
will gain three points, but will lose
nine points when his queen is swiftly
recaptured by the black queen on d8.

This rook is
defending the rook
on e8 and is ready
to recapture

This black rook will
be captured by the
white rook

◀ A fair exchange
If white decides to capture the black
rook on e8 with his white rook on e1,
black can easily recapture using his rook
on a8. This is a fair exchange – a rook for
a rook – as both rooks are worth five points.

MASTER CHALLENGE

To exchange or not to exchange?

It's good to get used to looking ahead
when you are playing a game and
being aware of the position of your
opponent's pieces. If your opponent
has a sneaky reply, then capturing a
valuable piece can sometimes lead
to disaster. Have a look at these two
boards and see if you can work out
whether the next move will lead to a
good, bad, or fair exchange for white.

1. Is it a good idea for the white
rook to capture the queen on e5?
Or will white end up worse off?

2. Should the white knight capture the
rook on c5 or on f6? Which capture
will gain the most points for white?

Developing your pieces

At the start of a game when you first move your pieces, you are said to be "developing" them. The four central squares are extremely important in this development and you should always try to attack or occupy these squares, as this allows your pieces to control a large area of the board.

◄ Controlling the centre of the board
The white bishop in the centre of the board can move to 13 different squares covering every part of the board, whereas the black bishop on the edge of the board can only move to seven different squares on his right. The white bishop is almost twice as powerful as his black counterpart.

Black needs to bring out his d7 or e7 pawns to release his back row pieces

Developing to control the centre
1 In the starting position, the pawns block in the two bishops. So on your first move, you should push the pawn in front of the king two squares forward, freeing the f1 bishop and giving the queen some space.

This bishop is now free to move into action

Develop like a demon

Developing well is an essential skill to learn since it sets your army up well for the game ahead. It can also give you the edge over your opponent, who may not be as quick as you to develop his pieces. Also remember that you are in a better position to confront your enemy if you have a multitude of pieces either occupying or attacking the central squares. Remember to centralize!

1. Should you move your white knight to a3 or c3? Remember that knights on the rim are dim!

2. Black has not developed his pieces well. Can you name three things he has done wrong?

MASTER TIPS

Play it safe

It is important to make sure that your pieces are safe. No one wants to lose their pieces because they've made a silly move. Examine carefully where you opponent's pieces are before you make your move. Always try to make a safe move to a square where you cannot be captured or where you are protected by your army. It is important to develop your pieces, but not at the expense of losing them.

1. White has just played d3. He didn't play d4 because his pawn would have been chopped off.

2. White moved his bishop to g5 and not f4, so as to avoid capture by the black e5 pawn.

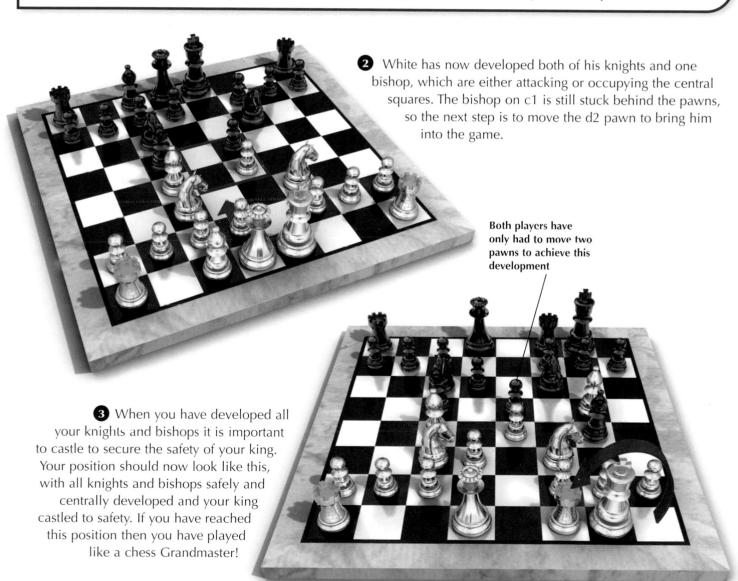

2 White has now developed both of his knights and one bishop, which are either attacking or occupying the central squares. The bishop on c1 is still stuck behind the pawns, so the next step is to move the d2 pawn to bring him into the game.

Both players have only had to move two pawns to achieve this development

3 When you have developed all your knights and bishops it is important to castle to secure the safety of your king. Your position should now look like this, with all knights and bishops safely and centrally developed and your king castled to safety. If you have reached this position then you have played like a chess Grandmaster!

Attack and defence

When you play chess you should always have a plan. You should always be able to give reasons for the moves that you make. Developing your pieces well is just the first stage in controlling the centre of the board, which in turn puts you in a strong position to launch some fierce attacks on your opponent.

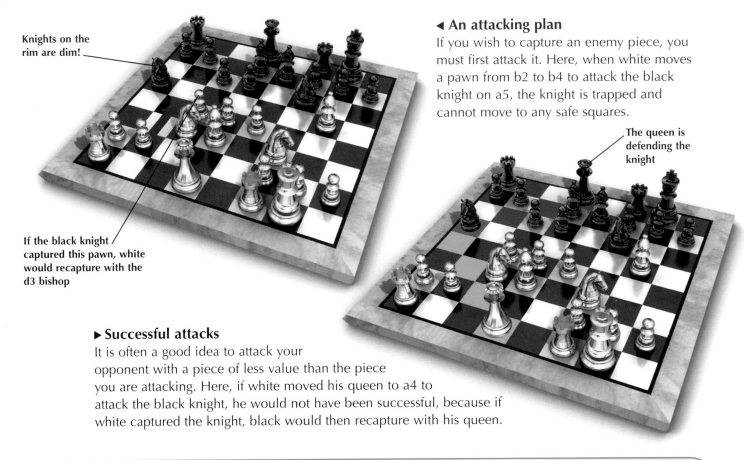

Knights on the rim are dim!

If the black knight captured this pawn, white would recapture with the d3 bishop

◄ An attacking plan
If you wish to capture an enemy piece, you must first attack it. Here, when white moves a pawn from b2 to b4 to attack the black knight on a5, the knight is trapped and cannot move to any safe squares.

The queen is defending the knight

► Successful attacks
It is often a good idea to attack your opponent with a piece of less value than the piece you are attacking. Here, if white moved his queen to a4 to attack the black knight, he would not have been successful, because if white captured the knight, black would then recapture with his queen.

Another successful attack

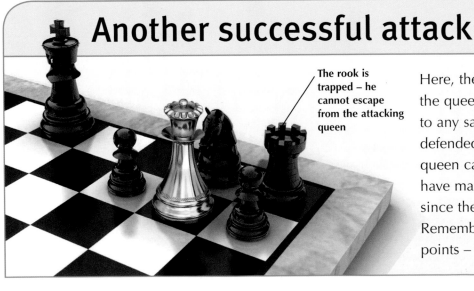

The rook is trapped – he cannot escape from the attacking queen

Here, the black rook is helpless against the queen's attack. He cannot move to any safe squares and cannot be defended by his own pieces. When the queen captures the rook, white will have made an advantageous capture since the queen cannot be recaptured. Remember that the queen is worth nine points – more than any other piece.

Loose pieces drop off

A wise man once said, "Loose pieces drop off", or LPDO for short. If your piece is loose, then it is not being defended by any of its army colleagues. Attacking loose pieces can be a very effective winning strategy and you should watch out for opportunities to chop off loose pieces at all times. You should also ensure that your pieces protect each other so that they are not loose.

1. The white queen has moved to g4. She is threatening the loose knight on b4 and checkmate on g7.

2. In this position, Qe4 or Qd3 threatens both the loose bishop on d4 and checkmate on h7.

Black needs to move his rook to defend the knight

▲ Defending a piece

Here, the white bishop is attacking the undefended knight on f6. If the knight moves, the bishop will capture the rook on d8. Black can defend the knight by moving her rook to d6. If white then captures the knight, black can recapture with her rook – a fair exchange.

▲ Defending your king

The most important piece to defend is, of course, your king. Here, the white queen is threatening checkmate on h7. Black can defend her king by moving her knight to f6 (Nf6). After which, capturing on h7 would lead to disaster for the white queen, as the knight would be able to take her.

Defend or die

You must protect your king against checkmate at all costs. How can you defend your monarch?

1. White is threatening Qg7 checkmate. If you were black, how would you stop the checkmate and launch a vicious attack of your own?

2. Here, black is threatening Qg2 checkmate. How can white defend his most valuable piece?

Four Move Checkmate

Scholar's Mate, which is also known as the Four Move Checkmate, is a great way to win some of your first games and it will really impress your friends.

1 First, move the pawn in front of your king two squares forward to open up lines for your queen and f1 bishop. Then bring your queen out diagonally as far as she can go – to h5. Next develop your bishop to c4. The queen and bishop are now both attacking the black pawn on f7.

The white queen is able to deliver checkmate because of the backup from the c4 bishop

The white king simply watches as his queen and bishop go on the attack

2 Black ignored the deadly threat to f7 and allowed the white queen to capture the pawn, giving a swift and deadly checkmate.

MASTER TIPS

Bash!

"Queen out, bishop out, bash!" is a quick and easy way to remember this checkmate. If you follow each step, you're bound to catch some people out with Scholar's Mate. However, it is vital that you develop your pieces accurately. If you miss out a move, or advance your queen or bishop to the wrong squares, your chance for a quick victory will be lost. You might even lose your queen.

1. White is not yet ready for the checkmate. He has not developed his backup bishop.

2. Here the b5 bishop has gone a square too far and can't protect his queen. He should be on c4.

Defending against Scholar's Mate

If you are being attacked by the Four Move Checkmate, you need to know how to stop it, as you don't want to become a victim of this cunning strategy. It's really very simple to prevent, as long as you pay close attention to your opponent's moves.

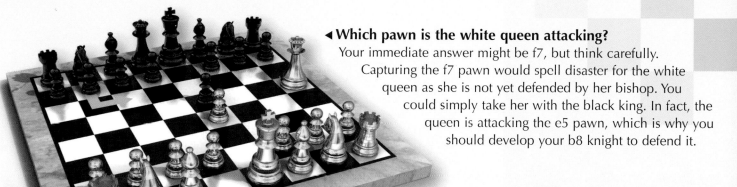

◄ Which pawn is the white queen attacking?
Your immediate answer might be f7, but think carefully. Capturing the f7 pawn would spell disaster for the white queen as she is not yet defended by her bishop. You could simply take her with the black king. In fact, the queen is attacking the e5 pawn, which is why you should develop your b8 knight to defend it.

► How can you stop the deadly mate threat?
You know that the white queen wants to capture on f7, so you have to stop her. The answer is to move the g7 pawn one square forward, blocking the path of the attacking queen and forcing her to retreat or die.

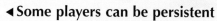

◄ Some players can be persistent
This time white is attacking f7 from a different angle. All black needs to do is block the threat by moving his g8 knight to f6. As long as you remember to block the queen, you will never fall for the Four Move Checkmate.

Two Rook Checkmate

Once you've chopped off all of your opponent's pieces, you will often find yourself in a position like this one, but how do you checkmate from here? You will quickly discover that in positions like these, it's almost impossible to checkmate the king in the middle of the board. It's much easier if you can force him on to one of the edges. All you have to remember are these three important rules.

❶ Form your barrier
This rook has formed a barrier. The king now cannot move forward as he would be moving into check.

The king is under attack and must move out of check

❷ Check with the other rook
If your barrier is in place, then you should check with the other rook, cutting off more squares from your opponent's king. The king must now move backwards to escape from check.

Trapped! ▶

Because the rooks can move quickly across the board the king is too slow to escape from them.

❸ Zoom your rook out of danger!

If your opponent's king ever attacks one of your rooks, you must move him out of danger. Make sure that your barrier is still in place and zoom him far away from the enemy king – if possible so he is diagonal to the other rook.

Two rook teamwork

Don't forget to look at the three rules while you complete this challenge. See if you can find white's best moves on the boards below.

1. It looks like the end is in sight for black. What should white do next?

2. Have you formed your barrier yet?

❹ Checkmate!

This process of forcing the king backwards will always lead to a checkmate like this. The black king is in check and cannot move to a safe square so it is checkmate.

Drawn games and stalemate

When you play a game of chess, you can win, lose, or draw a game. There are several ways in which a game is automatically declared a draw, but players can also decide to agree that their game is drawn, at which point they award themselves a half point each onto their score.

◀ Stalemate

The game is drawn and you are in stalemate when it is your move, you are not in check, but have no legal move. In this position it is black to move. The white queen prevents the black king from moving to any of the surrounding squares, but he is not in check. He also has no other legal move, so it is stalemate.

Not stalemate ▶

This is an almost identical position, except that black now has a pawn on a6. It is black's turn. The black king is not in check but is still unable to move. This time black can make a legal move. His pawn can advance one square forwards and it is therefore not stalemate.

MASTER TIPS

It has to be check for checkmate

Always keep your eyes peeled for stalemate traps, otherwise you may end up throwing away a winning position. Remember that if your opponent only has their king left on the board or if their other pieces cannot move, you should either make sure he can move to a safe square or that you have checked or checkmated him, otherwise a stalemate disaster may occur.

1. If the white queen moves to d7 it would be checkmate. Qe6 would, however, be a stalemate disaster.

2. The black king is almost out of moves, but he can move to f5. Always remember to check all your options.

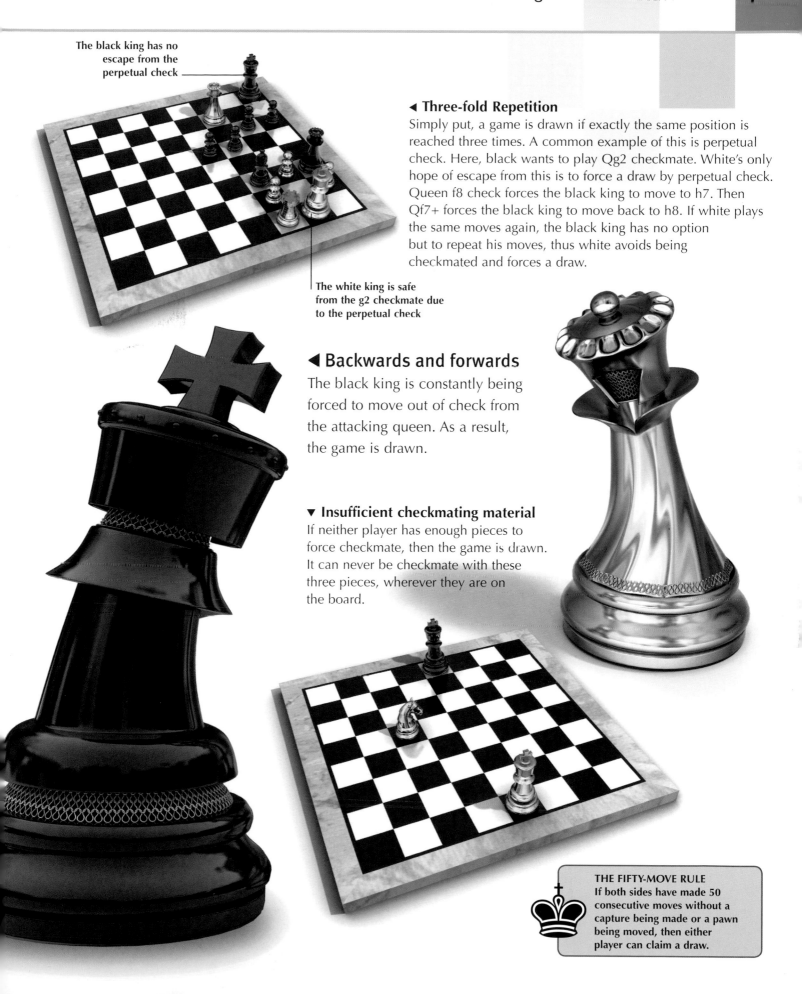

The black king has no escape from the perpetual check

The white king is safe from the g2 checkmate due to the perpetual check

◄ Three-fold Repetition

Simply put, a game is drawn if exactly the same position is reached three times. A common example of this is perpetual check. Here, black wants to play Qg2 checkmate. White's only hope of escape from this is to force a draw by perpetual check. Queen f8 check forces the black king to move to h7. Then Qf7+ forces the black king to move back to h8. If white plays the same moves again, the black king has no option but to repeat his moves, thus white avoids being checkmated and forces a draw.

◄ Backwards and forwards

The black king is constantly being forced to move out of check from the attacking queen. As a result, the game is drawn.

▼ Insufficient checkmating material

If neither player has enough pieces to force checkmate, then the game is drawn. It can never be checkmate with these three pieces, wherever they are on the board.

THE FIFTY-MOVE RULE
If both sides have made 50 consecutive moves without a capture being made or a pawn being moved, then either player can claim a draw.

King and Queen Checkmate

The queen is a very powerful piece, but when she is left alone, even she isn't able to checkmate without the help of her king. Once you've mastered the King and Queen Checkmate, the number of games that you win will shoot through the roof. Just follow these three steps.

1 Form a barrier with the queen, just as you would in the Two Rook Checkmate, to cut off the escape squares for the king.

The queen is a knight's move away from the enemy king

2 Move your queen so she is a knight's move away from your opponent's king, making sure your barrier is still in place and then pursue him. Here, the black king is moving one square diagonally, so that is precisely what the queen should do.

MASTER TIPS

Avoid stalemate

It is very important to keep your queen more than a knight's move away from the king once he has moved into the corner. Here it is black's move. He is not in check but has no legal move, so it is stalemate and the game is drawn.

The queen has stayed too close to the king and as a result it is now stalemate

Checkmate the king!

With practice, this checkmate will become second nature to you. As long as you follow the three simple rules and avoid dangers of stalemate, you will never go wrong.

1. Form the barrier.

2. Follow the enemy king.

3. Move in for the kill.

1. The black king has just moved from e8-d8. Where should the white queen move next?

2. There are three checkmates in this position. How many can you find?

③ The instant your opponent's king moves into the corner of the board, it's time to bring your king into action. You must leave your queen where she is or risk a stalemate disaster. The queen has the black king trapped and the white king has moved up to the crucial square, to back up his queen. White now has the option of delivering five different checkmates, none of which would have been possible without the aid of the king.

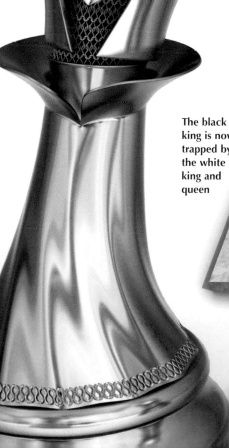

The black king is now trapped by the white king and queen

◀ The pursuing queen

The queen is always a powerful piece but in this instance she needs the backup of her king to checkmate her opponent.

CHAPTER FOUR:

Tactics

CONTENTS

Forks, pins, and skewers

Forks, pins, and skewers are some of the sneakiest tricks you can use against your opponent. These tactics can lead to winning one, and sometimes several, enemy pieces. Your tactical ability is important in your strength as a player because ultimately tactics will lead to winning the game.

◄ The fork

Where one piece attacks two or more pieces at the same time it is called a fork. When you fork pieces it can be difficult for your opponent to defend all of their men. Every piece on the board can fork – even the pawns.

MASTER TIPS

Absolute pin

The absolute pin is a really powerful tactic, as it paralyses the attacked piece. Here, if the d2 rook moves to a2, the black queen is lost, as she is unable to move away from the attack. She is absolutely pinned to her king on a8.

Notice that the d2 rook is backed up by the e2 rook.

◄ Kingpin

The black bishop attacks, pinning the white knight to the king – the knight cannot move or the white king will be in check.

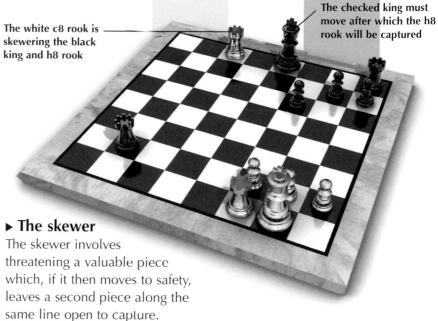

The white c8 rook is skewering the black king and h8 rook

The checked king must move after which the h8 rook will be captured

► The skewer

The skewer involves threatening a valuable piece which, if it then moves to safety, leaves a second piece along the same line open to capture.

▲ The pin

Another effective tactic is the pin. It is an attack on a piece which, if it tries to move, leaves a more valuable piece open to capture. Sometimes this can leave the opponent completely paralysed. The pinned piece is forced to stay where it is until the attacking piece moves or is captured.

MASTER CHALLENGE

Fork or skewer?

White is on the attack and can effect a fork or skewer in these situations. Can you tell which?

1. To where should the bishop move? Is this a fork, a pin, or a skewer?

2. Where should the white g5 knight move? Is this a fork, a pin, or a skewer?

Fried Liver

The strange name of this tactic actually comes from an Italian saying, "dead as fried liver", which perfectly describes the lethal result of this move if it is played correctly. Just like the Four Move Checkmate, it takes advantage of the weak square on f7.

❶ How do we reach Fried Liver?
It's really very simple. If you are playing white, you start with three sensible developing moves (e4, Nf3, Bc4). If black now plays Nf6, white can launch the fabulous Fried Liver attack.

It's vital that black has played this move, otherwise disaster strikes, as the black queen can simply chop your knight off

❷ Threatening a fork
White is now threatening Nxf7, capturing a pawn and forking two of black's major pieces – the d8 queen and the h8 rook.

MASTER TIPS

We love that liver!

A common question is "Why not take on f7 with the bishop instead of the knight?" Some people are tempted to capture with the bishop, because it will be check. However, when the king moves out of check, your attack is over and you have only won a pawn. In contrast, taking with the knight leads to winning a rook or a queen. Would you prefer to be a pawn or a rook ahead?

Remember, a check on its own doesn't achieve anything, the king will just move out of the way.

✓ Do
watch for an opportunity to use this effective tactic.

✗ Don't
launch the Fried Liver if your opponent has not developed his knight to f6.

Successful attack ▶
The white knight has manoeuvred himself into the position where he is forking the black queen and the black rook.

Defence against Fried Liver

If you are playing black in this game, you have a simple defence. After white has played Ng5, black should reply with pawn to d5. White will normally capture this with his e4 pawn, after which your best move is Na5, which will force the white c4 bishop off the diagonal where he is waiting to back up the attacking knight on g5.

❸ Fried Liver
When you first learn this trap, success is almost 100% guaranteed! The knight on f7 is now attacking two pieces and black only has time to save one. Notice that the c4 bishop is backing up the knight's position.

MASTER CHALLENGE

Attack and defence

Can you work out the answers to these two tricky Fried Liver questions?

1. It is white to move. Should he launch the fried liver with Ng5? Should the black knight still be on g8 in the Fried Liver?

2. Black has successfully blocked the path of the white bishop. What should black play now?

Sacrifice

A chess sacrifice can be described as a deliberate loss of material in return for an expected advantage. When you start playing chess, you are always aware of the points value of your pieces. However, in some very specific circumstances, it can be in your best interest to "sacrifice" or give away a piece. It's important to remember that chess is about checkmating your opponent's king, not hoarding pieces.

▶ An opening gambit

The Danish Gambit is a well known opening, which includes the sacrifice of two pawns. If you play these moves on your board at home, you will reach the position shown. Although white has given away two pawns, he has developed both bishops and has good control over the centre of the board, whereas black has lost just one pawn but the rest of his pieces remain on their starting squares.

White	Black
1 e4	e5
2 d4	exd4
3 c3	dxc3
4 Bc4	cxb2
5 Bxb2	

A checkmating sacrifice

❶ Here white gives up his queen in order to deliver a brilliant mate with his one remaining piece. White plays Qg8+, which forces Rxg8.

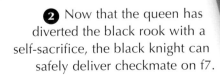

❷ Now that the queen has diverted the black rook with a self-sacrifice, the black knight can safely deliver checkmate on f7.

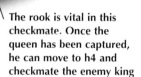

▶ Anastasia's Mate

Another checkmating sacrifice is known as Anastasia's checkmate. Here, the h5 queen, the e7 knight, and the e4 rook are involved. White performs the daring sacrifice Qxh7+, when black's only option is to recapture the queen with his king. Then Rh4+ is actually checkmate, as the king has been trapped by the rook and knight.

The rook is vital in this checkmate. Once the queen has been captured, he can move to h4 and checkmate the enemy king

The rook's move forces the white king to capture it and ends the game in stalemate

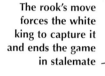

◀ A defensive sacrifice

Here, white is threatening three different checkmates – Qe7, Qf7, and Qh8. The situation looks hopeless for black, but Rd6+ saves the game. If the white king captures the rook, the black king is not in check, but has no legal move. It is stalemate. If the white king moves out of check, then the black rook can gleefully take the queen and the game is drawn, through a lack of mating material.

MASTER TIPS

Deflection

When you distract a piece away from defending another piece or square, this clever tactic is known as deflection. There are two different types of deflection shown here. The first one is a material-winning deflection where white will gain points from black. The second board demonstrates a cunning checkmating solution that will win white the game.

1. Which white rook deflects the h8 rook away from the defence of the h5 knight?

2. How can white checkmate the black king in two moves?

Back rank checkmates

In chess, a rank is a row of squares across the board. Your back rank is the row on which you place your king at the start of the game. Watch out, as a great many checkmates are delivered on the back rank of the board.

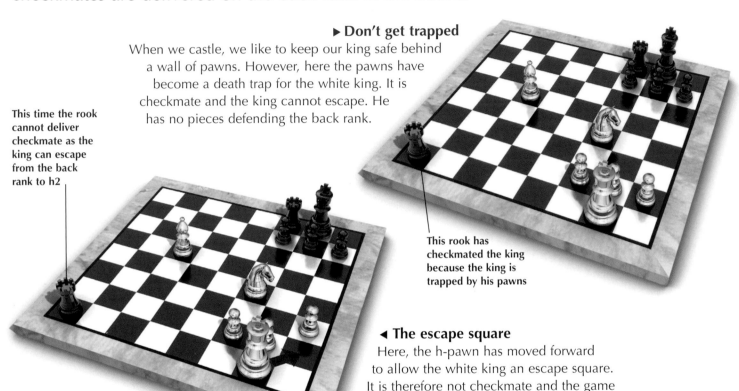

▶ **Don't get trapped**

When we castle, we like to keep our king safe behind a wall of pawns. However, here the pawns have become a death trap for the white king. It is checkmate and the king cannot escape. He has no pieces defending the back rank.

This time the rook cannot deliver checkmate as the king can escape from the back rank to h2

This rook has checkmated the king because the king is trapped by his pawns

◀ **The escape square**

Here, the h-pawn has moved forward to allow the white king an escape square. It is therefore not checkmate and the game can continue.

MASTER TIPS

Back rank blunders

Back rank checkmates can be delivered either by queens or rooks and can occur at any time during the game. So you should always be aware of the serious threat of a checkmate known as the submarine – or back rank checkmate – even if you think you've got it covered. Sometimes your opponent can cunningly block off your escape route!

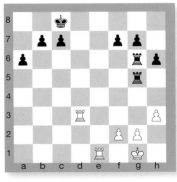

1. White rook to e8 would be checkmate, as the d3 rook has blocked off the d7 escape route.

2. The black king's escape square on h7 is covered by the white bishop on e4.

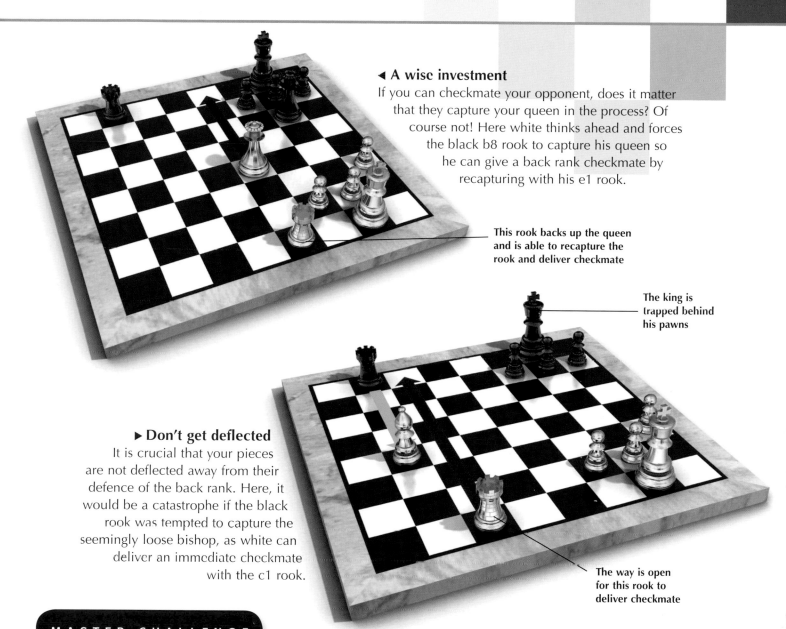

◀ A wise investment

If you can checkmate your opponent, does it matter that they capture your queen in the process? Of course not! Here white thinks ahead and forces the black b8 rook to capture his queen so he can give a back rank checkmate by recapturing with his e1 rook.

This rook backs up the queen and is able to recapture the rook and deliver checkmate

The king is trapped behind his pawns

▶ Don't get deflected

It is crucial that your pieces are not deflected away from their defence of the back rank. Here, it would be a catastrophe if the black rook was tempted to capture the seemingly loose bishop, as white can deliver an immediate checkmate with the c1 rook.

The way is open for this rook to deliver checkmate

MASTER CHALLENGE

Deflection or destruction?

In these seemingly innocent and equal positions, it is white's turn to move. Can you find the best continuation for white and cause devastation, either by winning material or checkmating black? Think about where your back rank mates are, which piece is stopping checkmate, and then deflect it (or them) away.

1. White is just moments away from achieving a back rank mate. What should be white's next move?

2. White has sensibly given himself an escape square on h2, but black has not been so clever.

G- and H-file checkmates

▲ **Using the g- and h-files**
You should attack black down these files. The f-file is easier for black to defend. In this typical castling position, the rook already defends f7.

▶ **Backup**
As you can see, the c2 bishop is providing the backup the queen needs to deliver checkmate. Without the backup of the bishop, the black king could capture the queen. He cannot capture the queen now because he would be moving into check.

It is no exaggeration to say that the powerful queen gives the majority of checkmates. If your opponent has castled kingside, your queen's checkmating attack will usually be launched down the g- or h-files, directly towards the enemy king.

The queen can safely checkmate the king

MASTER TIPS

Choose your checkmate

If your backup is missing or your opponent has defended against your attack, your checkmate will fail. It's always important to plan ahead in a game of chess and make sure you have backup for any moves you have planned, otherwise it could all go wrong if your opponent outwits you. Look at these positions carefully and find white's best moves.

1. Here, the backup for the h7 checkmate is missing, so white should play Ng5.

2. The black e6 knight currently prevents checkmate on g7, so white should simply chop it off. Rxe6.

Defending against the queen's attack

Recognizing when your king is in peril and knowing how to protect against this type of attack is crucial for chess success, as one tiny mistake can lead to your doom. Black's f6 knight is cleverly defending h7 against the queen's attack. If the knight had instead landed on g6, the game would be over, as the black queen could safely capture on h7 and deliver checkmate. Planning is everything and this time black has outwitted white.

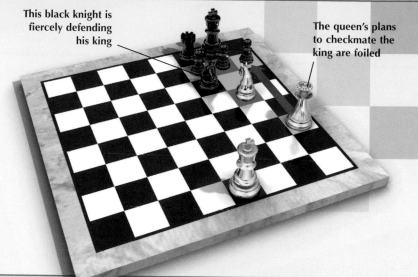

This black knight is fiercely defending his king

The queen's plans to checkmate the king are foiled

The black king must now move to h8

Delivering g-file checkmate

1 Here, the f6 bishop is defending the g7 pawn, foiling our plan of checkmate. So let's remove him with the d5 knight.

2 Now that the g-file defence has been removed, the white queen can play Qxg7 checkmate, as the white rook on g3 provides vital backup.

MASTER CHALLENGE

Good defending

Identifying weak squares and defending correctly is vital. Choose black's best move.

1. In this scenario, what should black do next to improve his defence? Should he play Nh5 or Bh5?

2. What move should black play here – Ng6 or Bf5?

The Greek Gift

The Greek Gift is a chess sacrifice that is frequently deadly. It refers to the tale of Troy, in which the Greek army left a giant wooden horse outside the gates of the city of Troy. Thinking it was a gift from the gods, the Trojans took the horse into their city and the Greeks then launched their surprise attack.

❶ Remove the defender
White's first task is to remove the defender of the black kingside – the f6 knight. Unless he wants to be captured by the e5 pawn, the knight is forced to move (Nd5).

❷ Offer the gift
Now white offers the Greek Gift and sacrifices a bishop for the pawn on h7 (Bxf7+). If the black king accepts the gift, then the race to checkmate him is on!

❸ Attack quickly
White is a bishop down and therefore vulnerable, so she has to move quickly and attack before the black king realizes his plan.

Fallen for the trap ▶
The black king has been tricked into accepting the sacrifice of the white bishop.

❹ Black retreats

White moves her knight (Ng5+) and the black king hurriedly retreats back behind his pawns where he thinks he will be safe (Kg8).

❺ The Queen arrives

The queen has come to join the fun (Qh5). In just a few moves, the position has changed dramatically. White is now threatening Qh7 checkmate and black must struggle to survive.

❻ Black gets desperate

In an attempt to stay in the game, black has chopped off the white g5 knight (Bxg5). White now has a choice of three different recaptures: Qxg5, hg5, or Bxg5.

❼ Bring in the backup

White recaptures with the h-pawn (hxg5). The h1 rook is now backing up the queen's h7 and h8 attacks. Black's only hope of survival is to move his f7 pawn to f5 to create an escape square for his king.

❽ Checkmate!

To block off the black king's last chance of escape, white advances her g-pawn to g6. Black is now powerless to prevent the checkmate.

Removing the defender

Your army is too valuable to leave in unprotected situations. Therefore it is important to keep your pieces defended. However, there are ways of removing your opponent's defending pieces that leave others open to attack.

Removing the defender of a piece

❶ Here, the black c6 knight is defending the d4 rook. When the white g2 bishop captures on c6, the black king must escape from check.

❷ The black b-pawn has captured the white bishop, but now that the defending knight has been removed, the white d1 rook can simply chop off black's d4 rook.

Removing the defender of a position

❶ The f6 knight prevents Re8 check, but here, the c3 bishop can remove the annoying defender with check (Bxf6+).

❷ The g7 pawn has recaptured the white bishop in retaliation, but now, as the e8 square is undefended, the white rook can move straight to it and skewer the black king and queen. The black king must move, after which white will take the black queen.

This white rook is backing up the rook on e8

Removing the defender of the king

1 Without his defensive forces, the king is frequently in serious trouble and here, it will lead to immediate checkmate. The white bishop takes the defending black f6 knight with check.

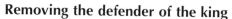

The white bishop moves to capture the knight

The white king is protected behind his pawns

2 The black queen immediately retaliates and captures the bishop. However, the white queen can now take the pawn on h7. The queen cannot be captured, the check cannot be blocked, and the king has no safe squares – it is checkmate.

MASTER CHALLENGE

Bash black into submission

It's time to get tough with black and remove his defending pieces. Here are two boards representing different types of removing the defender. Can you find the brilliant move in each position? Removing the defender is an extremely useful tactic, which, once you have mastered it, can be used with lethal results on your powerless opponent. You have to be quick to see the possibilities.

1. White would love to be able to capture the black rook – but how to get rid of the black knight?

2. Have a good look at the white knight. Which square would he like to move to? Who must he remove?

Seventh Heaven

The seventh rank is deep in your opponent's territory and is where your opponent's pawns begin their slow journey. If you can get both your rooks on to that seventh rank you will gain a lot of power, as they can work together and gobble up any other piece in their path!

▶ Dual control
Here, the white rooks are able to zoom up and down the seventh rank and chop off all the pawns.

Pawn carnage ▶
All in all, rooks on the seventh rank give you much greater chances to win.

Creating chaos

The white rooks are ideally placed on the seventh rank and are poised to chop off the enemy pieces. Even in such a powerful position, you still have to be careful about the position of your opponent's pieces.

1. If white wants to win a pawn, what should his next move be?

2. Black is about to get a shock. How can white now checkmate in three moves?

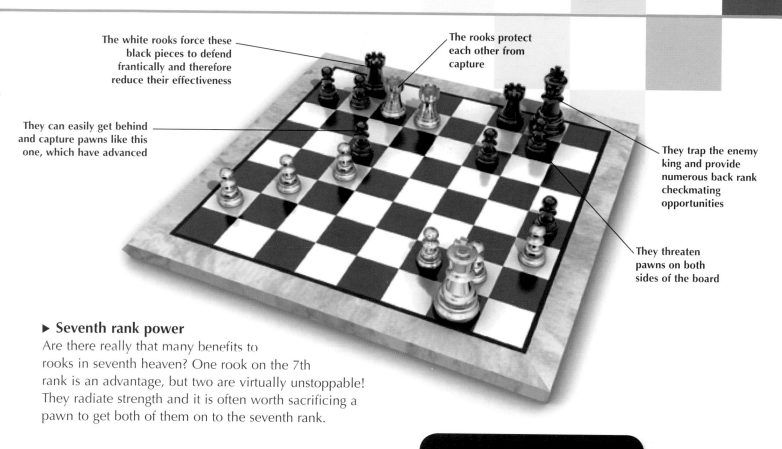

The white rooks force these black pieces to defend frantically and therefore reduce their effectiveness

The rooks protect each other from capture

They can easily get behind and capture pawns like this one, which have advanced

They trap the enemy king and provide numerous back rank checkmating opportunities

They threaten pawns on both sides of the board

▶ Seventh rank power

Are there really that many benefits to rooks in seventh heaven? One rook on the 7th rank is an advantage, but two are virtually unstoppable! They radiate strength and it is often worth sacrificing a pawn to get both of them on to the seventh rank.

MASTER TIPS

Double trouble

If you put both your rooks on the same file (up and down the board), or on the same rank (sideways across the board), you often double their strength, as they back each other up and can chop off a lot of pieces. If you manage to reach the seventh rank your opponent is in for trouble!

Here, because of the valuable backup from the e1 rook, white is able to play Re7+.

When white moves to the seventh rank he can attack both the king and the c7 pawn.

Discovered attacks

When you hit your opponent with a discovered attack, it is as if you have ambushed them. One of your own soldiers leaps out of the way to reveal that an attacking piece has been craftily hiding behind him all along.

Double discovered attack ▶
The piece that leaps out of the way is often able to pose a threat itself. Here, Bh6 discovers a near fatal attack on the black position. White threatens both Qg7 checkmate and the capture of the black queen by the rook on e2. Black cannot halt both of these threats and must immediately lose his queen or the game.

◀ Double discovered attack with check
Double discovered attacks often involve discovered checks. Bishop to b5 is a discovered check. It reveals a powerful attack on the undefended black queen by the white queen. Black must get out of check, after which, white will simply chop his queen off. Beware that Loose Pieces Drop Off!

MASTER TIPS

Double discovered checks

These can be the most vicious of all onslaughts. When your opponent finds himself in double discovered check he must attempt to move his king. Sometimes it can be checkmate immediately, but more often this type of assault allows you to zoom in for the kill! Look at these great examples of double discovered checks and checkmates and see how cleverly white has positioned himself.

1. Look how the rook and the bishop are lined up against the black king. Bc5 is a double discovered checkmate.

2. White has sacrificed his queen for a forced checkmate. Ne6 forces black to play Ke8, then Rd8 is checkmate.

Conquering the copycats

1 Here, black has copied white's first two moves but now it all starts to go wrong. The white knight has just captured black's e5 pawn. If black continues to mirror with Nxe4, his position will fall apart.

2 Black has moved his knight and white has now played Qe2. If black copies again with Qe7, white can capture the black knight and protect the white knight on e5. If the black knight suddenly realizes that things aren't going his way and retreats to f6, white has a fantastic discovered attack, which wins the black queen.

3 Nc6+! This reveals a discovered check on the black king by the white queen. The knight on c6 also attacks the black queen on d8. Black must get out of check immediately, after which his queen will be captured either on d8 or e7 when she blocks the check.

Discover your potential

When your pieces are lined up against the enemy forces a discovered attack can frequently be on the cards. Can you find the best move for white in these two positions?

1. Black has blocked the discovered check by playing Qe7. Would you capture her with your queen or your knight and why?

2. Can you find the discovered attack white can launch to win the black queen?

The Duke of Brunswick game

This unusual and briliant game was played in the Grand Opera House in Paris in 1858. Paul Morphy, an American chess genius, had been invited to the opera by the Duke of Brunswick and Count Isouard. During the interval, they challenged him to a game of chess and he politely accepted. Try playing this game on your own board and look out for the tactics and themes covered in this book as you play.

Black's bishop is trapped by the d6 pawn

White has opened a path for his queen and his bishop

❶ The opening moves
Morphy (playing white) makes his opening moves by bringing out a pawn (e4) and a knight (Nf3). The Duke (playing black) responds with two pawns (d5 and e6).

The black bishop had a clear path into the game

The f4 bishop is pinning the f3 knight to the queen

White moves his pawn to d4 before capturing on e5

❷ Controlling the centre of the board
Morphy advances his d4 pawn and continues with his sensible policy of controlling the centre of the board. The Duke develops his bishop (Bg4) which Morphy follows by capturing the e5 pawn (dxe5).

❸ A sequence of captures

The Duke retaliates by capturing the f3 knight, but Morphy is too quick and recaptures by bringing out his queen (Qxf3). The Duke then takes Morphy's d5 pawn (dxe5). Material gains are level at this point.

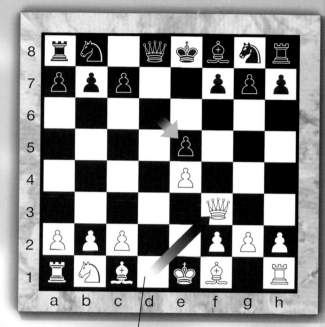

White brings his queen into battle

Black cannot allow white to take this pawn or it will lead to checkmate

❹ An early checkmate threat

Morphy was keen not to miss the second half of the opera so he threatened a sneaky checkmate. He brings out his white bishop (Bc4) but the Duke blocks this with his knight (Nf6). Morphy now brings out his queen (Qb3) launching a double attack on b7 and f7.

This pawn is now protected by the queen

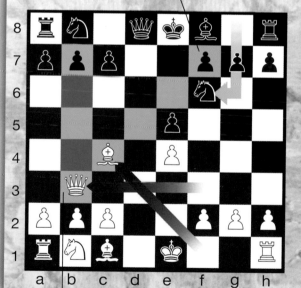

Both the f7 and b7 pawns are under attack by the queen

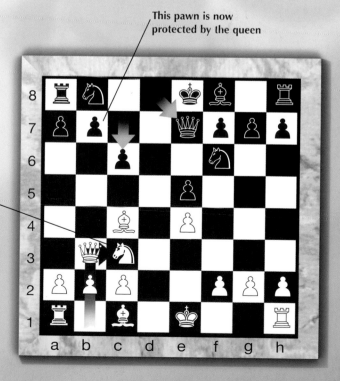

White brings out his other knight

❺ Deepening development

The Duke hastily moves his queen to defend f7 against the checkmate threat (Qf7). But instead of capturing the b7 pawn, Morphy continues to develop and brings out his other knight (Nc3). The Duke then brings out another pawn (c6).

6 The start of a devastating attack
Morphy brings out his other bishop (Bg5). The Duke launches an unwise attack with another pawn (b5) which is immediately captured by Morphy's c3 knight (Nxb5).

The bishop is pinning the f6 knight to the e7 queen

Black's pieces are not well developed and squeezed into the corner

White on the attack 7
The Duke now takes the b5 knight with his c6 pawn. But the victory is short-lived as Morphy confidently recaptures the pawn with his bishop, putting the king into check (Bxb5+). The Count is forced to defend with his other knight (Nd7). White is now fully on the attack. Notice how white is attacking both of black's knights with his bishops.

Black's rook and bishop are still trapped

This rook is free to move along the back rank

8 Castle and attack
Morphy castles queenside (0-0-0), immediately attacking down the d-file with his rook. The Duke is forced to defend his knight with his a8 rook (Rd8).

This rook is waiting for his chance to pounce

❾ White launches a clever sacrifice…
Morphy bravely sacrifices another piece by capturing the black knight with his rook (Rd7), which he knows the Duke will immediately recapture with his d8 rook (Rd7).

❿ …and then another…
Morphy brings his other rook in to action (Rd1). The Duke, keen to release his f6 knight from his pin, offers an exchange of queens (Qe6). Morphy turns down the offer and instead captures the rook (Bxd7+).

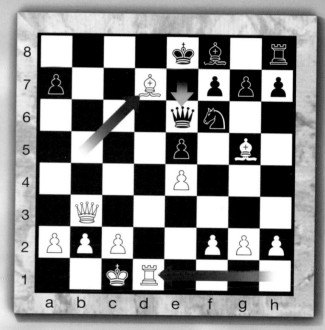

The knight was forced to capture the queen

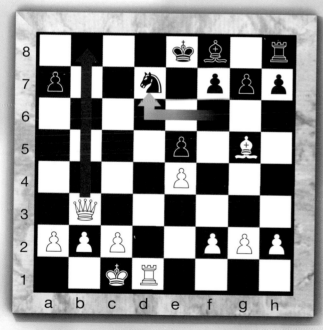

⓫ …and yet another!
Black must recapture the bishop with his f6 knight (Nxd7). The white queen then moves straight to b8 in a daring sacrifice, forcing a brilliant checkmate (Qb8).

⓬ Checkmate!
The Duke has no option but to capture the queen with his knight (Nxb8). This now leaves the d-file open for the d1 white rook to deliver a swift checkmate on (Rd8+).

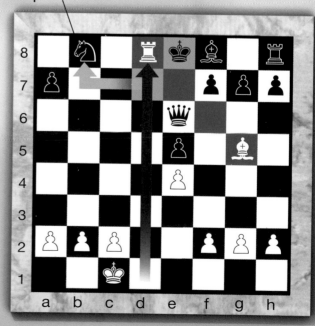

Glossary

Adjudication
A way of deciding the result of an unfinished game. A strong, impartial player evaluates the final position and assigns a win, draw or loss depending on best play by both players.

Adjust or *j'adoube*
If your piece is not in the centre of a square you may wish to adjust it's position, without being forced to move it because of the "touch move rule". You should say "I adjust" before touching the piece.

Backup
Your pieces are said to back each other up when they protect each other.

Barrier
Normally formed with a queen or rook. It serves to block off squares from your opponent's king.

Blunder
A very bad move.

Capturing
When you capture your opponent's pieces, you land on their square and they are then removed from the board.

Castling
When you castle, your king moves two squares towards your rook and the rook then jumps over and lands next to the king.

Central Squares
The four squares in the very centre of a chess board are described as the central squares.

Check
When the king is attacked by an enemy piece, we say that he is in check.

Checkmate
If your king cannot escape from check, then you are in checkmate and your opponent has won.

Chop off
Another way to describe capturing a piece.

Deflection
When you distract a piece away from defending another piece or square.

Developing
When you first move your pieces at the beginning of a game, you are said to be developing them.

Discovered attack
When a piece moves and uncovers an attack on an enemy piece.

En passant
A special move that is an alternative method of capturing with a pawn.

En prise
A French phrase meaning that a piece is unprotected or loose.

Exchanging
When you capture a piece and your opponent recaptures, you have exchanged pieces.

Files
There are eight files on a chess board, running up and down the board.

Fork
When one piece attacks two or more enemy pieces at the same time.

Gambit
A gambit is a chess opening where one player sacrifices material (usually a pawn) for another type of advantage. Gambits may either be accepted or declined.

Grandmaster
An expert chess player.

Knights on the rim
The rim is the edge of
the board.

Loose pieces
A piece is loose, and likely
to be captured, if it is not
protected by another piece.

Major pieces
Rooks (worth five points) and
queens (worth nine points).

Material
If you have captured more
valuable pieces than your
opponent, you are said to
have "a material advantage"
or be "material up".

Minor pieces
Knights and bishops (each
worth three points).

Open lines
A line (rank or file) can be
described as open when it is
not blocked by either friendly
or enemy pawns.

Opponent
The person that you are
playing against.

Piece value
Every piece is allocated a value,
which depends on its strength.
The more powerful a piece is,
the higher its points value.

Pin
An attack on a piece which, if
it tries to move, leaves a more
valuable piece open to capture.

Queening
Also known as promoting.
When your pawn reaches the
other side of the board you
can immediately change it
(or queen it) into a knight,
bishop, rook, or queen.

Ranks
There are eight ranks on a chess
board, running side to side
across the board.

Sacrifice
A deliberate loss of material
in return for an expected
advantage over your opponent.

Scholar's Mate
Another name for the
Four Move Checkmate.

Scoresheet
You can "score" or write down
your moves on a scoresheet,

using chess notation to record
your progress in the game.

Skewer
An attack on a valuable piece,
which when it moves leaves a
second piece open to capture.

Stalemate
If you are not in check, but
have no legal move then you
are in stalemate and the game
is drawn.

Tactics
The science and art of
effectively manoeuvring
your chess pieces.

Tempo
If you take two moves to
accomplish what can be done
in one move (or three moves
where two moves are enough,
etc.) you are said to have
lost a tempo, or time.

Touch move
If it is your move and you
touch one of your pieces,
you must move it (if you
can). If you touch one of your
opponent's pieces, you must
take it. When you take your
hand away from your piece,
you must leave it there.

Solutions

Where moves are listed in notation form, white always moves first, for example:

White	Black
1. Rxa4	Rxa4

p.15: The rook
1. c8.
2. The white rook should move from a1-a6-e6-e3-c3-c4

p.17: The bishop
1. The rook on a7
2. The bishop can move to seven squares and capture the black rook on f6.

p.19: The queen
1. The rook on c3
2. The bishop on d8

p.21: The knight
1. g5 – a black rook
2. The knight has many different routes to capture the pawns. One route is Nb1-c3-b5-c7-e8-f6-d7

p.23: The pawn
1. The best capture is exd5, taking the black queen and gaining 9 points. If you capture the bishop on f5, you only gain 3 points.
2. You should queen your pawn by moving to b8.

p.25: The king
1.

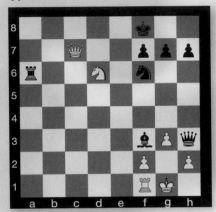

Qxf7 is checkmate, as the knight backs up the queen. Qb8+ allows the black king an escape square on e7. Qd8+ can be blocked by Ne8, but does lead to checkmate. Qc8+ leads to disaster for white, as the black queen can capture on c8.

p.31: Piece value and exchanging
1. Rxe5 is a good exchange for white. He would gain 9 points but only lose 5 points when black recaptures, Rxe5.
2. Nxc5 is the best capture (5 points), as Nxf6 can be recaptured by the g-pawn (5-3=2 points)

p.32: Developing your pieces
1. Centralize your knight to c3.
2. a) The kingside knight is on

the rim – h6.
b) He has moved four pawns in the opening.
c) The king has moved to e7 for no reason.

p.35: Attack and defence
1. Rg8 protects g7 and attacks the white queen and the vulnerable g-file. Black can now hope for a checkmate on g2.
2. Pawn to f3 blocks the path of the backup bishop and prevents the checkmate.

p.39: Two Rook Checkmate
1. Rg8 is checkmate, whereas Rh8 removes the barrier and allows the king to escape.
2. The rook on a6 is in danger, so you should zoom him away from the king to g6.

p.43: King and Queen Checkmate
1. Qf7 follows the king and is a knight's move away from the d8 king.
2. Qg7, Qe8 and Qd8 are all checkmate.

p.47: Forks, pins and skewers
1. If the bishop moves to e4 he will pin the black queen to the king.

2. The white knight should capture the pawn on f7 where he will fork the black queen and the h8 rook.

p.49: Fried Liver

1. Here, Ng5 would be the incorrect option, as black could simply capture the knight with his queen, Qxg5.
2. Black should play Na5, forcing the backup bishop off the important diagonal.

p.53: Back rank checkmates

1. Qxd2 wins the black rook or leads to checkmate. If black recaptures Qxd2, then Re8 is checkmate
2. Rxa4 either wins the bishop or leads to a back rank checkmate.
   1. Rxa4   Rxa4
   2. Qxa4

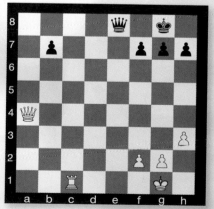

2. ...   Qxa4
3. Rc8+   Qe8 (forced)
4. Rxe8 checkmate

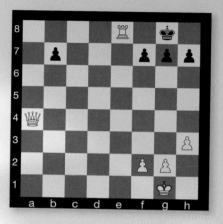

p.55: G- and h-file checkmates

1. Nh5 defends against the checkmate on g7. Bh5 allows Qg7 checkmate.
2. Bf5 defends against the checkmate on h7. Ng6 does not.

p.59: Removing the defender

1. 1. Bxc6+ bxc6 is best
      2. Rxb4 wins the black rook
2. Rxc8 removes the defender. Nf5+ forks the queen and king.

p.60: Seventh Heaven

1. Rxb7 wins a pawn.
Rxg7 loses a rook to Bxg7.
2. 1. Rxg7+   Kh8
      2. Rxh7+

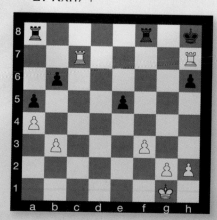

2. ...   Kg8
3. Rxg7 checkmate

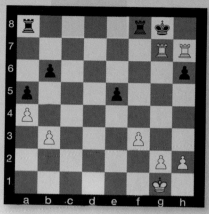

p.63: Discovered attacks

1. White should capture the queen with the knight on c6. This wins 6 points – a knight (3 points) for a queen (9 points). Qxe7+ would be a mistake, as the black bishop would recapture the white queen.
2. Bxh7+ discovers an attack by the white queen on the undefended black queen.

Index

Acknowledgements

The publisher would like to thank the following for their kind permission
to reproduce their photographs:
(Key: a-above; b-below/bottom; c-centre; f-far; l-left; r-right; t-top)
Alamy Images: Visual Arts Library (London) 4bl. Corbis: Ken Kaminesky
5br. Freer Gallery of Art, Smithsonian Institution, Washington DC: 4cl.
Getty Images: Reportage 5tr.

All other images © Dorling Kindersley
For further information see: www.dkimages.com

Thanks also to Sylvia Potter for proofreading and indexing.